FASCINATING FACTS

FOR

D1273032

10

YEAR OLD KIDS

A Message From the Publisher

Hello! My name is Hayden and I am the owner of Hayden Fox Publishing, the publishing house that brought you this title.

My hope is that you and your young comedian love this book and enjoy every single page. If you do, please think about **giving us your honest feedback via a review on Amazon**. It may only take a moment, but it really does mean the world for small businesses like mine.

Even if you happen to not like this title, please let us know the reason in your review so that we may improve this title for the future and serve you better.

The mission of Hayden Fox is to create premium content for children that will help them increase their confidence and grow their imaginations while having tons of fun along the way.

Without you, however, this would not be possible, so we sincerely thank you for your purchase and for supporting our company mission.

Sincerely,
Hayden Fox

Copyright by Hayden Fox - All rights reserved.

In no way is it legal to reproduce, duplicate, or transmit any part of this document by any means which includes graphically, electronically, or mechanically, including but not limited to photocopying, recording, taping, or by digital storage. Recording of this publication is strictly prohibited and any storage of this document is not allowed unless with written permission from the publisher. All rights reserved.

There are about 18 minutes of actual action in a baseball game, even though they can last for 3 hours on average.

BABE RUTH was one of the first athletes to become a true celebrity and was known for his extravagant lifestyle, which included fast cars, parties, and fine dining.

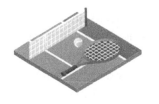

The first Wimbledon tennis tournament was held in 1877 and only included men's singles matches.

The highest-scoring NBA game in history took place on December 13, **1983**, when the Detroit Pistons beat the Denver Nuggets 186–184 in triple overtime.

Usain Bolt, the **FASTEST** man in history, holds world records for the 100 meters, 200 meters, and 4x100 meters relay, and is the only sprinter to win gold in all three events at three Olympic Games.

The first ever baseball game to be broadcast on radio was on August 5, **1921**, between the Pittsburgh Pirates and the Philadelphia Phillies.

The first Olympic marathon race in 1896 was won by a Greek runner named SPYRIDON LOUIS, who was working as a water carrier at the time.

The first recorded game of ice hockey was played in Montreal in 1875, using a ball instead of a puck.

There have been three Olympic Games held in countries that NO LONGER EXIST.

GREECE is the only country to have participated in every Olympics under its own flag.

Only **11** goalies have scored a goal in the history of the NHL, with the first coming in 1979 and the last in 2020.

The PGA record for highest score on a par-4 is a whopping **16**, set by Kevin Na in 2011.

RASHEED WALLACE had his 2004 Detroit Pistons championship ring resized to fit his middle finger.

Alaska, South Dakota, and Maine are the only states to never send a school to the **NCAA** tournament.

CRICKET is the second-most popular sport in the world, with over 2.5 billion fans.

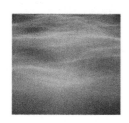

In the 1962 NFL championship game, the Green Bay Packers and New York Giants played in what is known as the "FOG BOWL," where the field was so foggy that players and officials could barely see.

SAMMY SOSA has three of the eight 60-home run seasons in baseball history.

The longest recorded point in tennis history took 29 minutes.

The first-ever documented boxing match took place in 1681 in Britain, between the Duke of Albemarle's butler and butcher.

The fastest goal ever scored in a soccer match was by Hakan Şükür of Turkey, who scored just **11 SECONDS** into a match against South Korea during the 2002 World Cup.

FOUR presidents have been on the cover of Sports Illustrated: John F. Kennedy, Gerald Ford, Ronald Reagan (twice) and Bill Clinton.

The shortest player in NBA history was Muggsy Bogues, who stood just **5 FEET 3 INCHES** tall.

Despite receiving invitations, **ENGLAND** didn't participate in the first three World Cups.

Joe Gibbs is the only coach to win the Super Bowl with **THREE** different quarterbacks.

The highest-scoring NHL game in history took place on December 11, 1985, when the Edmonton Oilers beat the Chicago Blackhawks 12-9.

The speed of sound in air is SLOWER than the speed of light, meaning we will see the lightning first, before hearing the thunder.

Thunder is the sound caused by lightning. The intense heat generated by lightning causes the air to rapidly expand and contract, producing a shock wave that we hear as THUNDER.

Hailstones can reach the size of grapefruits or even larger. The largest hailstone ever recorded fell in Vivian, South Dakota in 2010, measuring **8 INCHES** in diameter and weighing 1.94 pounds.

To become a **METEOROLOGIST,** you will need a Bachelor of Science Degree in either Meteorology or Atmospheric Sciences.

Meteorologists get to travel all over the **WORLD**, researching facts about weather and climate and reporting back.

There are SiX main types of factor used to describe weather: wind, humidity, precipitation, temperature, atmospheric pressure and cloudiness.

The word meteorology comes from two GREEK words, 'meteroros' and 'logia', meaning "in the sky" and "study".

Instead of using SALT, which can actually harm the environment, some cities have started using surprising methods to help clear the roads from snow. Did you know that beer waste, pickle brine and beet juice can all melt ice?

Some snow is better for making snowballs! Snowflakes that fall through temperatures above 0 °C will melt a tiny bit around the edges, these flakes stick together easily and make snowballs perfect for an epic snowball fight!

The first weekly weather forecast was printed in the London Times, in

1861.

A **MiCROBURST** is a sudden, powerful downdraft of air that can cause significant damage on the ground. Microbursts are most commonly associated with thunderstorms and can produce wind gusts of up to 168 miles per hour.

Fogbows are similar to rainbows, but they appear as white or gray arcs in FOGGY conditions. They are sometimes called "ghost rainbows" or "white rainbows."

In 2009, a week long sandstorm in the Middle East was so huge that it could be seen from

SPACE!

Hot weather plays a big role in wildfires. DROUGHT can lead to the perfect conditions for a fire. The leaves and underbrush covering the ground trap heat from the sun, which can spark the fire.

HURRICANES are tropical storms that begin life at sea. The largest hurricane ever recorded was in 1951 in the northwest Pacific Ocean. Named Typhoon Tip, this hurricane was almost half the size of the USA!

Some of the windiest places on Earth can be found in **MIDWEST** America – Chicago is even known as The Windy City.

BALL lightning is a rare phenomenon that occurs during thunderstorms, where a bright, glowing ball of light appears to float in the air. Scientists still don't fully understand what causes it.

Facts about climate and weather are possible to record thanks to The World Meteorological Organization. This UN agency is in charge of verifying figures like the hottest day ever recorded.

HEAT WAVES are caused
by air trapped by high pressure systems, where the air is forced downwards and can't rise into the cooler upper atmosphere.

Seasons, ocean currents, weather and climate are all driven by the connection between the SUN and

EARTH.

Satellite temperature data collected over seven years, showed the consistently hottest place on Earth to be the Lut Desert in Iran. The highest temperature the desert reached was a staggering **70.7°C (159.3°F)!**

The **FUJITA** scale, also known as the F-scale, is a system for rating tornado intensity based on the damage caused by the tornado. The scale ranges from F0 (weakest) to F5 (strongest).

In 2003, a heatwave so intense turned grapes into **RAISINS** before they were picked from the vine.

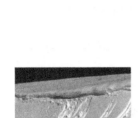

Snow ROLLERS are rare meteorological phenomena that occur when snow is picked up by the wind and rolled into cylindrical shapes. They are often found in open, hilly areas and can be as large as several feet in diameter.

The shortest war in history was between Britain and Zanzibar in 1896 and lasted only

38 MINUTES.

The waves in the ocean are caused by the gravitational pull from other celestial bodies, most notably the MOON and SUN.

Elephants can communicate through **SEISMIC WAVES** and can "hear" each other's calls from miles away.

There are more possible iterations of a game of **CHESS** than there are atoms in the observable universe.

The longest word in the English language is **189,819** letters long and is the chemical name for the protein Titin.

PEACHES are members of the almond family.

KETCHUP was once sold as a medicine.

 A group of flamingos is called a **FLAMBOYANCE.**

Cows give more milk when they listen to **MUSIC.**

The world's oldest piece of chewing gum is over **9,000** years old.

"E" is the most common letter and appears in 11 percent of all English words.

COPPER door knobs are self-disinfecting.

The moon has
MOONQUAKES.

"NEW CAR SMELL" is the scent of dozens of chemicals.

 Rabbits can't **PUKE.**

Chewing gum boosts
CONCENTRATION.

 Children's medicine once contained
MORPHINE

There are multiple decorated war hero **DOGS.**

A **CROCODILE** can't stick its tongue out.

The only letter that doesn't appear in any U.S. state name is **Q.**

Koalas have **FINGERPRINTS.**

The **TONGUE** is the strongest muscle in the human body relative to its size.

The oldest known fossils are **3.7 BILLION** years old and were found in Greenland.

The longest wedding veil ever made was longer than 63 football fields.

Some planets produce
DiAMOND RAiN.

The world's largest snowflake on record was 15 inches wide and 8 inches thick.

Space is a hard vacuum, meaning it is a **VOID** containing very little matter.

The center of a comet is called a **NUCLEUS.**

The largest planet in our solar system is **JUPITER.**

NEUTRON STARS come into being when massive stars collapse.

Astronauts have to **EXERCISE** for two hours every day to keep their muscles and bones strong in space.

Jupiter's Great Red Spot, which rotates once approximately every six days, is an anti-cyclonic **STORM** 22° south of the planet's equator.

Stars don't TWINKLE until their light passes through Earth's atmosphere.

The Hubble Space Telescope has taken over a MILLION pictures of space.

Our Milky Way galaxy is 2.5 million light-years away from the nearest other galaxy, ANDROMEDA.

Space is completely silent because there is NO AIR for sound waves to travel through.

There are over **200 BILLION** galaxies in the universe, by current estimates made by Hubble space telescope.

Galaxies not only come in different sizes, but also different **SHAPES.**

If the galaxy is too far away to distinguish individual stars, astronomers find SUPERNOVAE, which are much brighter than ordinary stars. They use those to measure that distance.

SATURN is the second largest planet in our solar system.

The planets in our solar system are separated into the planets of INNER solar system, and the OUTER solar system.

FOR 10 YEAR OLDS

 The pressure on the surface of Venus is as high as it is at the depth of **1 KILOMETER** in Earth's oceans.

Saturn's **RINGS** are made up of tiny ice particles.

 Every year there are at least 2 lunar (Moon) eclipses, but solar eclipses are much **RARER.**

The SEASONS we experience are due to the tilt of the Earth's axis, which makes certain areas get more sunshine at the different parts of its revolution around the Sun.

The Moon's gravity is 1/6 of Earth's.

There are FIVE officially recognized dwarf planets in our solar system: Pluto, Eris, Haumea, Makemake, and Ceres.

FOR 10 YEAR OLDS

One day on Venus is LONGER than one year on Venus.

Saturn has **SEVEN** distinct rings.

COMETS are made of ice, dust, and gas. When they get close to the Sun, they start to melt and form a long tail that can be seen from Earth.

TIC TACS got their name from the sound they make when they are tossed around in their container.

It snows **METAL** on planet Venus! There are two types that have been found: galena and bismuthinite.

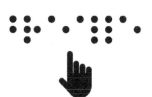

The majority of blind people in the U.S. and the U.K. **CANNOT** read braille.

FOR 10 YEAR OLDS

Sloths only go to the bathroom
ONCE A WEEK.

Most female cats prefer
using their **RiGHT** paw
while males are more likely to
be left-pawed.

Over **200** people have died
climbing Mount Everest since
1922.

FOR 10 YEAR OLDS

Some ants can carry objects up to **50** times their own body weight.

The world's largest rubber band ball weighs over **9,000** pounds.

The longest ever recorded flight by a paper airplane was over **27** seconds.

FOR 10 YEAR OLDS

"TSUNDOKO" is a Japanese word for the habit of buying too many books, letting them pile up in your house, and never reading them.

SAMSUNG means "three stars" in Korean.

The Guinness World Record for the time longest spend searching for the Loch Ness Monster is held by Steve Feltham who camped at Loch Ness for **28** years.

BEES actually have knees.

In Japan, there is a hotel staffed entirely by ROBOTS.

Santa Claus was issued a pilot's license from the U.S. government in **1927.**

FOR 10 YEAR OLDS

 **COWS** have best friends and get stressed when separated from them.

There is an insurance policy issued against **ALiEN** abduction. Around 50,000 policies have been sold, mainly to residents of the U.S. and U.K.

Disappointment Island is an uninhabited island in **NEW ZEALAND**

VOLVO invented the three-point seatbelt, then gave the invention away for free. They decided it was too important of an invention to keep to themselves.

The world's smallest mammal, a Bumblebee Bat, weighs about the same as a U.S. DIME.

A 17-year old with DWARFISM played the 8-year-old Grinch in The Grinch (2000).

The **BRiTiSH POUND** is the world's oldest currency still in use at 1,200 years old.

All the paint on the Eiffel Tower weighs the same as **TEN** elephants.

The world's largest **BOOK** is 13 feet tall and over 6 feet wide.

In 1992, a shipping crate containing 28,000 RUBBER DUCKIES fell overboard. They washed up around the world for the next 20 years.

A PRiME number is a number that can only be divided by 1 and itself (for example, 2, 3, 5, 7, 11, etc.).

The symbol for INFiNiTY (∞) represents a quantity that is larger than any number.

The number **Pi** and the pies we eat are linked.

SERGEY BRIN, co-founder of Google, studied mathematics (and computer science) at university.

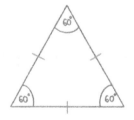 The sum of the angles in a triangle is always **180** degrees.

William Shanks calculated Pi to 707 decimal places but made a mistake on the **528TH** digit.

If you shuffle a deck of cards properly, it's more than likely that the exact order of the cards you get has **NEVER** been seen before in the whole history of the universe.

You can cut a cake into 8 pieces by using only **3** cuts.

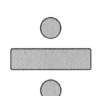 The symbol for division (÷) is called an **OBELUS.**

The numerator of a **FRACTION** is the top number, and the denominator is the bottom number.

13 There are **13** letters in both "eleven plus two" and "twelve plus one".

2.46 The **DECIMAL POINT** is used to separate the whole number from the fractional part in a decimal number.

BAKING is both mathematical and delicious!

The **LEGO** factory produces around 36,000 pieces of LEGO every minute.

An average bathtub holds **42** gallons of water.

An Olympic-sized swimming pool has **660,253** gallons of water.

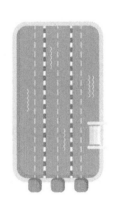

The radius of the moon is approximately **1,079.6** miles

 Light from the sun takes approximately **8 MINUTES** and 15 seconds to reach us on Earth.

The **MEDIAN** is the middle value in a set of numbers when they are arranged in order.

 The **MODE** is the value that appears most frequently in a set of numbers.

The **RANGE** is the difference between the highest and lowest values in a set of numbers.

A baseball diamond is a perfect rhombus, which is a type of shape known as a PARALLELOGRAM.

 PROBABILITY is the study of the likelihood of events occurring.

STATISTICS is the study of collecting, analyzing, and interpreting data.

In medieval times, the Japanese used to dye their teeth **BLACK.**

Most carrots used to be **PURPLE**, and it wasn't until the 17th century that most of them became orange.

The **HUBBLE** telescope used a black and white camera to capture pictures in the past.

BLACK is the absence of color, and WHITE is the presence of all colors.

There are seven colors in a rainbow: red, orange, yellow, green, blue, indigo, and violet (ROYGBIV).

FOR 10 YEAR OLDS

Veterinarians used to believe that dogs saw only in black and white, but studies suggest that they actually do have some COLOR vision.

Many common colors used for dog toys are HARD for a dog to see.

Colors can affect our moods and emotions. For example, BLUE can have a calming effect.

FOR 10 YEAR OLDS

As a deterrent to poachers, South African authorities inject a strong **RED** dye into rhino horns which is clearly visible and poisonous to humans.

The only green over red stoplight in USA world is in **SYRACUSE,** New York because some persistent local Irish kids didn't want the red (British) above green (Ireland).

Green and red peppers are not distinct varieties. Rather, green peppers are simply **IMMATURE** versions of red peppers.

Colors can also have cultural and historical meanings. For example, **RED** is often associated with luck in Chinese culture.

The **MARGHERITA** pizza owes its name to Italy's Queen Margherita, who in 1889 visited the Pizzeria Brandi in Naples.

Some animals can see colors that humans **CAN'T.**

ESPN won an Emmy for the creation of the superimposed yellow line representing the first down line for American football games.

BLUE -eyed people probably have a single, common ancestor, who had a genetic mutation between 6,000 and 10,000 years ago.

The **FILIPINO** flag is flown with the red stripe up in times of war, and blue stripe up in times of peace.

The primary colors are **RED,** YELLOW and **BLUE.**

Most people dream in color, but for those who grew up watching monochrome television, there is a good chance that they also dream in

BLACK AND WHITE.

American school buses are yellow because you see YELLOW faster than any other color.

Germany's racing color is **SILVER** because, in 1934, one of their cars was barely overweight, so they just scrapped the paint off, leaving the silver body. The car managed to win and the color stuck.

The color **PINK** doesn't exist in the rainbow, it is actually a combination of red and violet.

The first synthetic dye, called Mauveine, was created in 1856 and was a **PURPLISH** color.

The most complex eyes throughout the animal kingdom belong to the **MANTIS SHRIMP**, who can manipulate light polarization throughout its entire visible spectrum.

Sharks kill fewer than 10 people per year. Humans kill about **100 MILLION** sharks per year.

Some people can see more colors than others due to a condition called **TETRACHROMACY**, which is caused by having an extra type of color receptor in the eyes.

The **TONGUE** of a blue whale weighs more than an elephant.

A group of pandas is called an
EMBARRASSMENT.

CHAMELEONS can move their eyes in two different directions at once.

The **MANTIS SHRIMP** has the world's fastest punch.

Female lions do **90** percent of the hunting.

Ducks can SURF.

FOR 10 YEAR OLDS

Pigeons can do **MATH.**

Baby kangaroos are called **JOEYS.**

 Dogs have way **FEWER** taste buds than humans.

Koalas sleep up to **20 HOURS** a day.

A group of ferrets is called a
BUSINESS.

Octopuses can taste with their **ARMS.**

Hippos secrete a pinkish-red fluid which acts as a natural **SUNSCREEN.**

An elephant's trunk has over **40,000** muscles in it.

Alligators can grow for more than **30** years.

Male horses have way more **TEETH** than their female counterparts.

Giraffes have **BLACK** tongues.

Giraffes can clean their ears with their tongues, which are over 18 INCHES long.

 **BATS** are the only mammals capable of sustained flight.

Narwhal **TUSKS** are really an "inside out" tooth.

 The tongue of a blue whale is so large that **50** people can stand on it.

FOR 10 YEAR OLDS

Baby Tasmanian devils make life-long **FRiENDSHiPS.**

Some snails have **HAiRY** shells.

Penguins can jump up to **6 FEET** in the air.

Apples float in water because they are **25%** air, meaning they are less dense than water.

HONEY never spoils if stored properly.

 Technically speaking, BANANAS are a berry but strawberries are not.

We humans share 60% of our DNA with BANANAS.

The world's largest chocolate bar weighed over **12,000** pounds.

One stalk of celery has NEGATIVE calories because it takes more calories to eat and digest than it contains.

PiNEAPPPLES used to be so expensive that people would rent them to display at parties.

The world's most expensive spice is **SAFFRON.**

Popcorn was first eaten by Native Americans over 5,000 years ago.

Ketchup used to be sold as
MEDICINE.

Broccoli is a **FLOWER.**

The world's most popular spice is
BLACK PEPPER.

The world's most expensive mushroom is the white truffle, which can cost over $2,000 per pound.

The world's most expensive fruit is the Japanese Yubari cantaloupe, which can cost over $20,000 for a pair.

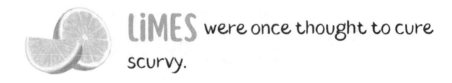 LiMES were once thought to cure scurvy.

The world's largest chocolate chip cookie weighed over **40,000** pounds.

Some people are allergic to the protein in wheat, which is called **GLUTEN.**

 In ancient Greece, throwing an **APPLE** to a woman was a proposal of marriage.

The world's largest food fight takes place in Bunol, Spain, where over **100 TONS** of tomatoes are thrown.

PENNSYLVANIA is home
to the "mushroom capital of the world".

 The oldest known recipe in the world is for beer and is over **4,000** years old.

Your food is **ALLOWED** to contain trace of insects.

Fruits and vegetables are **LESS** nutritious than they used to be.

The world's largest cheese sculpture weighed over **2,000** pounds.

Bananas are

RADIOACTIVE.

In 18th century England,

PINEAPPLES were a

status symbol.

The American Civil War was fought from **1861 TO 1865** and resulted in the end of slavery in the United States.

During the Great Depression, people made clothes out of food **SACKS**. People used flour bags, potato sacks, and anything made of burlap.

The first airplane was invented by the Wright brothers in **1903.**

The Eiffel Tower in Paris was built in **1889** and is one of the most famous landmarks in the world.

During World War II, a Great Dane named JULiANA was awarded the Blue Cross Medal. She extinguished an incendiary bomb by peeing on it!

The MAYANS were skilled mathematicians and astronomers who developed a complex calendar system.

There were female Gladiators in Ancient Rome! A female gladiator was called a GLADiATRiX, or Gladiatrices. They were extremely rare, unlike their male counterparts.

The **ROARING TWENTIES** was a period of great cultural and social change in the United States.

WORLD WAR ii was fought from 1939 to 1945 and involved many of the world's major powers.

The **VIKINGS** were expert sailors and explorers who traveled far and wide, raiding and trading in Europe, Asia, and North America.

TUG OF WAR used to be an Olympic sport! It was part of the Olympic schedule between 1900 and 1920 and occurred at 5 different Summer Olympic Games. The nation to win the most medals in this was Britain with 5 medals, then the USA with 3.

The Mona Lisa is a famous painting by Leonardo da Vinci that is over **500** years old.

The fall of the Soviet Union in **1991** marked the end of the Cold War.

Before alarm clocks and way before smartphone alarms, there were people called knocker-uppers who would literally KNOCK on people's windows to wake them up in time for work.

The COLD WAR was a period of tension between the United States and the Soviet Union that lasted from the end of World War II until the early 1990s.

The BERLIN WALL was a symbol of the Cold War that divided the city of Berlin in Germany from 1961 to 1989.

The **CiViL RiGHTS** movement in the United States was a struggle for equal rights for African Americans that took place in the 1950s and 1960s.

Adolf Hitler helped design the Volkswagen **BEETLE.** The iconic bug-like car was designed as part of a Hitler-revived German initiative to create an affordable and practical car that everyone could own.

NELSON MANDELA was a South African leader who fought against apartheid and became the country's first black president.

 Iceland has the world's oldest parliament in history. Called the ALTHING, it was established in 930 and has stayed as the acting parliament of Iceland since then.

Alexander the Great named over 70 cities after himself. Alexander the Great conquered over 2 million square miles of the Earth's surface all by the time he was 30.

 The INTERNET was invented in the 1960s and has since transformed the world.

CLEOPATRA was the first member of her dynasty to speak Ancient Egyptian. She was also able to speak 8 other languages including Ancient Greek, Ancient Iranian, Ancient Parthian, Syriac, Ethiopian, Troglodytae, Hebrew and Arabic.

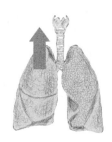

Your **RIGHT** lung can take in more air than your left.

There are about **6 BILLION** bacteria in the human mouth.

Each of us has around 10,000 taste buds on average.

The human eye can distinguish 10 **MiLLiON** different colors.

The chemical compound in the body, which causes feelings of ecstasy (phenylethylamine), is also contained in **CHOCOLATE.**

FOR 10 YEAR OLDS

 The average adult has around
100,000 hairs on their head.

The average human has around
5 MiLLiON sweat glands.

 Our noses can remember upto
50,000 different scents.

A person will produce enough saliva in their lifetime to fill two SWIMMING POOLS.

The **CHERNOBYL** disaster was a nuclear accident that occurred in Ukraine in 1986 and had far-reaching consequences.

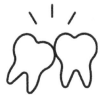

The **ENAMEL** on our teeth is the hardest substance in our body.

Your brain uses **20%** of the oxygen that enters your bloodstream.

The **ARAB SPRING** was a series of protests and uprisings that took place across the Middle East and North Africa in 2011.

Most of us don't remember many of our dreams and the average length of most dreams is only **2-3** seconds– barely long enough to register.

The brain itself cannot feel
PAIN.

73% of the brain is **WATER.**

The **BLACK LIVES MATTER**
movement is a social movement that
campaigns against violence and
systemic racism towards black people.

FOR 10 YEAR OLDS

 Our small intestine is around **22 FEET** long.

The tiny bones in your ear are smaller than a grain of **RICE.**

 Your hair grows faster in **WARM** weather.

GRETA THUNBERG is a
Swedish activist who campaigns for action on climate change and has inspired young people around the world to take action.

The human body is estimated to have

60,000 miles of blood vessels.

SIMONE BILES is an American
gymnast who has won numerous Olympic and world championship medals and is considered one of the greatest gymnasts of all time.

 The largest internal organ is the **LIVER.**

You get a **NEW** stomach lining every three to four days.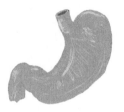

 The World Wide Web was created in **1989** by Sir Tim Berners-Lee.

The first email was sent in 1971 by Ray Tomlinson.

By 2025, the number of social media users in the world is expected to grow to 4.41 BiLLiON users.

 The INTERNET was originally created as a way for researchers to share information.

In **1990**, the first search engine, "Archie Query Form", was launched.

4 BiLLiON email users were registered worldwide in 2020.

The first YouTube video was uploaded on **APRIL 23, 2005.**

Яндекс

42% of people in Russia use the
YANDEX search engine.

76% of people in China use the
BAIDU search engine.

2.7% of Internet users use the
YAHOO! search engine.

The internet is estimated to use about **10%** of the world's electricity.

0.88% of Internet users use the **DUCKDUCKGO** search engine.

2.5% of Internet users use the Bing search engine.

The internet was originally called the **ARPANET.**

As of 2021, more than **500** hours of video are uploaded to YouTube every minute.

The **INTERNET** is a global network of computers that are connected to each other.

 The "WWW" in website addresses stands for "World Wide Web".

Google's original name was "BACKRUB".

 The first domain name ever registered was Symbolics.com on MARCH 15,1985.

The first popular web browser was called Netscape Navigator, which was launched in 1994.

The ETHERNET cables used today for the internet were invented in 1974 for telecom networks.

 The "404" error message appears when a webpage cannot be found or does not exist.

The first online banner ad appeared on the website of Wired Magazine in 1994.

The INTERNET has been credited with revolutionizing the way we communicate, learn, work, and socialize.

The hashtag symbol (#) was first used on Twitter in 2007 to group tweets by topic.

The first webpage is still
ONLINE.

The internet is more than

11,500 days old.

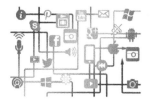

The average growth rate of
internet users is **4.8%** per year.

Leave Your Feedback on Amazon

Please think about leaving some feedback via a review on Amazon. It may only take a moment, but it really does mean the world for small businesses like mine.

Even if you did not enjoy this title, please let us know the reason(s) in your review so that we may improve this title and serve you better.

From the Publisher

Hayden Fox's mission is to create premium content for children that will help them expand their vocabulary, grow their imaginations, gain confidence, and share tons of laughs along the way.

Without you, however, this would not be possible, so we sincerely thank you for your purchase and for supporting our company mission.

Made in United States
North Haven, CT
08 April 2023

35203407R00059